MW00964213

Every Emotion

Every Emotion

Hebridean Poetry

George Carle

George Carle
26th June 2019

Writers Club Press
San Jose New York Lincoln Shanghai

Every Emotion
Hebridean Poetry

All Rights Reserved © 2000 by George Carle

No part of this book may be reproduced or transmitted in any form or by any means, graphic, electronic, or mechanical, including photocopying, recording, taping, or by any information storage retrieval system, without the permission in writing from the publisher.

Writers Club Press
an imprint of iUniverse.com, Inc.

For information address:
iUniverse.com, Inc.
5220 S 16th, Ste. 200
Lincoln, NE 68512
www.iuniverse.com

ISBN: 0-595-16274-6

Printed in the United States of America

To my dear children Erin and Ethan who brought joy to my life.

Epigraph

But pleasures are like poppies spread,
You seize the flow'r, its bloom is shed;
Or like the snow falls in the river,
A moment white—then melts for ever

Robert Burns, from *Tom o' Shanter*

Contents

ANGUISH

LOVE

List of Published Poems

Where Have My Children Gone? *The Consuming Flame*
                             Anthology Writer's Cauldron

Sadly Sleeps my Son   *In the Shadow of the Faith*
                             Anthology Chamber of Dreams
                             Nature's Echoes Anthology

Beyond Passion   *Nature's Echoes Anthology*

Life after Death   *Nature's Echoes Anthology*

Where have my Children Gone? *Nature's Echoes Anthology*

Moods   *Voice and Verse*

Separation   *First Time*

Take Me   *Writer's Cauldron*

Beyond Passion   *Writer's Cauldron*

Bumblies Begone   *Krax*

Rivers of Rain   *Writer's Cauldron*

Absent Son   *Writer's Cauldron*

Rhyme of Love   *Writer's Cauldron*

The Seeds of Barley Love   *First Time*

I am no Mortal Man   *First Time*

The Woman of Whispering White Voice and Verse

Introduction

Throughout my life I have enjoyed reading and listening to poetry. I even had the notion that I might be able to write it! It seems strange for a man of forty-six to suddenly find poetry—but this is exactly what happened in my case. My marriage broke up two years ago and my wife left suddenly, taking my two dear children with her. Living on a remote and isolated island intensified my sadness and I required treatment for depression. During this illness I started to write poetry and found I enjoyed it.

Separation is acutely painful, and although my marriage had been over for some time I missed my wife's presence dreadfully. After living with someone for nearly twenty years and having two children in the process, sudden separation is difficult to cope with. The poetry in this collection refers to the state of my marriage and my reaction to separation. The poem "Separation" refers to my feelings on opening my bedroom door immediately after my family's departure.

Loss of my children was the hardest part of all. My daughter was aged thirteen and attending Oban High school, living in the hostel for island children. Her departure wasn't so noticeable but painful nevertheless. My son was five and constantly around. I just could not believe he had gone. It's perhaps my children poems that express most of my pain at the time and reflect how deeply I felt about the loss. The poem "Orange Boy and Me" was scribbled down on an old newspaper during a train journey. The orange refers to the colour of my son's anorak and for me this poem is particularly poignant

As might be expected, this was a very turbulent time and I experienced considerable changes in mood, including depression. My mind was in turmoil and my anguish poetry reflects this. The poem "Moods" was written when I was considerably depressed and refers to the stark contrast between elation and depression. The poem hints at the fact that individuals with emotional lability may be very sensitive and creative. The poem demonstrates what a profound effect mood can have on an individual's life.

I very much enjoy writing love poetry and this is why there are eighteen poems in this category. Some were written from imagination but a few refer to real life events.

"The Seeds of Barley Love" was inspired by a visit to Aberdeenshire to see my father. While travelling by car between Ellon and Aberdeen I could not help but notice the barley fields waving in the wind and the poem came into my head.

I do not attend church and I am not a deeply religious man, but I do have an inner faith and enjoy writing poems about it. "Circular God" was written one Sunday morning as I sat in my living room with the sun streaming through the window. I could hear the local church bell ringing and a religious poem seemed appropriate. This particular poem was written in about five minutes and needed very little revision.

There is something quite fascinating about death and several poems in this category are included. The poem "A Time to Die" was written as a tribute to a very good friend and patient. Before his final illness I used to visit him once a week as a friend. He was full of stories and indeed one of his tales inspired a poem about the hill where public hangings used to be carried out. The poem I wrote was of course "Hangman's Hill"

Living on Coll is far from easy. Many services taken for granted on the mainland are just not available. Summers are on the whole enjoyable but winters full of wind and rain. The very small community has its own set of problems. There is no constant police presence on the island and this encourages lawlessness. My poem "An Island Life" is a rather jaded, tongue-in-cheek look at what life is like on Coll

Friends and family forever accuse me of being egocentric, so it is no surprise to see three such poems in the collection. The one I personally identify with is "I am no Mortal Man." There was a bridge and I did stand on the middle of it pondering my past and future lives. I had started writing poetry and a few poems had been accepted for publication in poetry magazines. In the grand scheme of things I did see myself as a poet who achieves immortality.

Humour is all around us and to find it all we have to do is look for it. I like to think that I have a good sense of humour and I suppose it shows in the humorous poems included in this section. The poem "Clicking and Whirring" referred to the computer on my desk in the surgery. I wanted to see if I could make up a poem about this intrinsically boring piece of equipment. I wanted to be descriptive throughout the poem and only reveal its identity with the last line.

Ageing is a reality, a fact of life. We are born, we age and then we die. There are three poems dealing with age and my favourite is "Father of his Flock." This was written as a tribute to my father who is in his eighties and suffers from Parkinson's disease and other medical problems. The theme of this poem was to contrast my father's present appearance with his appearance as a younger man. The words "withered brain" were perhaps rather harsh—but my father was delighted with the poem!

Narrative poetry is out of fashion, but three such poems are included. "Supper for the Sharks" was written one day travelling by ferry between Coll and Oban. I remember it was a beautiful day and the sun was blazing down. I imagined I was on a pirate ship and someone was being made to walk the plank into a shark-infested sea.

Some six poems did not fit into recognised categories. "The Wahine" refers to a beautiful Polynesian or Maori woman. One night while surfing the WWW I found a site with a wahine racing back and forth at the top of the screen with a direction saying "Hit the wahine and win!" I did not know what the word meant, but I looked it up in the dictionary and wrote the poem!

One night I was looking at the picture above the fireplace and this inspired me to write a poem. The picture is of Ophelia sitting on a bough above a pond with lily pads. She seemed desperately sad—as is the lady featured in the poem "A Sort of Justice."

"Rivers of Rain" was written one wet and rainy day when I was looking at rain running down the window pane.

George Carle

1

SEPARATION

Separation

An empty house, an empty room
The room we knew so well
But never more shall share
Those reassuring times again
Sadness fills my very soul
My eyes are full of tears
Forget forget that is best
Lest dwelling on it me destroy.

Not for Him

——————— ∞ ———————

Not for him the happy hearth and home
The warming wife and welcome child to greet
Blissful dreams domestic for some endure
But this hapless breed of being he was not
Conceptual gifting was his curse
Mere men to stand aside while he dominated
Their lives by colossal power of mind
And when this measure failed did manipulate
Them whilst knowing what he did was wrong
All he touched were treated with disdain
Even the worn out woman, mother of his child
Until a day when all in hell were loosed
An orgy of womanizing steeled his spouse
Who fled and stole his cherished child
A father to his child but seldom husband man
This once powerful man now racked and ruined
Had to draw on all resolve he did possess
He nor wife did know till then that strength
That he possessed came from his family ties
Now all is gone, his aura dies.

Companion marriage

Did you ever wonder
What I was all about?
Did you ever care
Enough to say
Why is he so?
Living separate lives
Bedding you no more
Knowing all the time
We were miles apart
Talking different language
With no common thought
Comforting companions
Ending in disaster
I knew it surely would
Painful so extreme
The breaking of my heart
Raw my feeling then
Kinder with each day
Healing almost anything
Time has shown the way.

Dissecting the Parting

And when we both agreed
It was the time to part
We knew not where to go
Inward tangled lives
Painful leaving lingered
Oh the cooling passion
Now there's only hate
No more sweet embraces
Seeking separate lives
So urgently they wait

Our union was but sham
So clear it was to all
We never had a chance
This outcome meant to be
On this let us agree.

Loving and Leaving

———— ∞ ————

After all the loving and the leaving
Never more shall we be one
Sorrows new each day brings
Piercing painful every one
Leave not such loving long
Lest loving loses all
Needing loving new and now
Separate shall we journey on.

2

CHILDREN

Paternal pleas

———— ∞ ————

Let me hear my children's voices
Let me hear each one
I used to hear them every day
Now I hear not one

Let me see my children
Let me see each one
I used to see them every day
Now I see not one

Let me have my children
Let me have each one
I used to have them every day
Now I have not one.

Son of a Poet

He is of me and of my seed
Germinating those years ago
A living breathing flesh
Now that boyish being
I call joy who left me
Never of his own will
Returns like a sad past
And then I remember when
We had that special bond
An easy understanding
No word we spoke
There was no need
As if we knew always
What came next
And what to do
But distance separates
Our link of harmony
I worship him still
But now from afar
And empty are my days
Without his gentle ways.

Orange Boy

———— ∞ ————

Orange boy and me
Riding on the train
The train that takes him from me
With a rattling rough refrain

Oh stay with me forever
And fill each empty day
My wonder child from heaven
Who must not go away.

Where have my Children gone?

Suddenly, painfully all gone
My world is lost, I'm all alone
I miss their pretty presence so
More than they will ever know
On I go without their fame
Those darlings at birth who came
And filled my life with joy
I love you girl and boy.

Sadly sleeps my Son

— ∞ —

Sadly sleeping lay my son
Heavy eyelids drugged by sleep
Pale-faced and serenely still
Carried on some wave of dreams
Why so sad my brilliant boy?
Do you know your father still?
He will come to you again
But curse the empty days between.

Two Worlds

I cannot give you now
What I could give you then
Our worlds have moved apart
Wide waters wash between
But we fine breed of men
Transcend such parting waves
To rise above fierce foam
And grasp that bond of kin
It shall not last forever
I daily strive to right
A poet has fine words
But together we shall fight.

Where Shall My Love Be?

———— ∞ ————

Look for me when the sun is high
And there are no clouds to see
Look for me in the sun-kissed sleep
There my children's love shall be

Look for me when the moon is high
And there are no stars to see
Look for me in the dream-filled sleep
There my children's love shall be

Look for me when the spirit's high
And there is no flesh to see
Look for me in the angel's sleep
There my final love shall be.

A Lost Daughter

*My daughter does not want me
It seems too hard to bear
I love her very deeply
And always want her there
I know her scars are painful
And cause her great concern
I hope that time will heal them
And both of us may learn.*

3
ANGUISH

Free Me

Give me freedom from this place
That rancours sore with me
And where all hell broke loose
And I the price did pay
I'm tinged with lonely sadness
That grips this being so
And causes me to doubt
Whether ever I shall go.

Fire and Ashes

Up and up I go reaching for the stars
Intoxicated by excess I lust for life extreme
It feels too good it can't be real
A dream a dream it must be so
Cloaked awakening, devil despair
That tears my splendid world apart
Extinguishing my joy my hope
And tempting death the ashes blow away.

Moods

---∞---

Shall he ever be well again?
Must moods control his life?
Despairing black that grips him so
Or joyous rainbow like
Call it deep emotion
A man of great excess
So sensitive and creative
Yet poorly understood
Leading those who follow
A gifted man he should.

Now and Then

My mind is sick
My body weak
Problems all I see
And fear the future so
Yet a time there was
When I was strong
And did not doubt the way
My star was bright
The light so clear
My destiny assured.

A Lost Life

Wrecked by manic madness
His life did take away
Replaced by something different
Forever now that way

Seeming somehow primal
Perceived perhaps to say
The past is but a wistful dream
The future's spawned today.

Deranging Demons

Believe me my brothers we know what we are
We walk with the angels and cry like a child
Our lives like an ocean of breakers and foam
We can't stop them now they must surely go on
God gave us the anguish but also our minds
We all feel the pain as it slices once more
But we're not the worst we know this is so
Crazed souls are detained and never may go.

Tormented Times

Weaker now
Weaker in the mind
Than I care to be
Emotional eggshells all the way
Situations in the past
Then were happy in harmony
Now agony and piercing
Like my emotional mind
Can cope no more
Each instance building
Into a massive mess
Of mental weakness
And ugly uncertainty
I know not where it takes me
But I am resolute
I shall endure
Though it may take
All the strength in me
To bear this fearsome flood
Of demon doubt
And in so doing
Rise again renewed.

Fire and Vapour

———— ∞ ————

Those crimson days of scarlet
When life was uncontrolled
No effort needed then
As through life I strolled

Restless in the body
Motion made me ache
The need for constant movement
Submission, my mistake

Drugged sleep of Morpheus
Alas could never be
Wilful ways of wakefulness
Perhaps possessed you see

A mind so stuffed with wonder
How could I find my way?
Frenetic thoughts flew frequent
And anguished every day

The engine now revs normal
So futile firing fast
High octane pump is dry
Euthymic man at last.

Return From the Wilderness

So weary in that wilderness
I've wandered in my gloom
Clothed in ragged garb
The berry flesh my food

Lean brown the body borne
A starved and weathered man
My mind so pure in thought
A life that is but naught

Transformed I see the reason
I need to leave this dearth
Self rescue from such limbo
To embrace my kindred men.

Fear

Fear the light
Feels too bright
Fear the night
Hurts my sight
Fear my right
Makes me fight
Fear my might
Makes me bite.

A Poet's Song

Sifting through the anguish
The agony and pain
I came across my song
A lyrical refrain

Born bearing blemishes
I never could deny
They made my life more difficult
God knows I had to try

All my life I fought to win
Against such unfair odds
Many times lesser men
Were favoured with the nods

Life in a world of prejudice
How hard to make one's mark
But I did find the light
While others found the dark.

Emotional Man

And when it was all over
He tried to start anew
But the tears of regret
Washed away like rain

He'd never be the same
An ethos grossly changed
If he could live it over
I doubt he'd do the same

Boisterous bad behaviour
Wrecked his tender life
An elevated mood
Blew his world apart

Like the roller coaster
Always up or down
Notorious are the moods
Of this sad and happy clown.

4
LOVE

Woman of Whispering White

Wondering in his half sleep
Would she come again?
Did she visit others?
To share her love with them

Content in warmth he lay
Relaxed, his body calm
Drifting into deeper sleep
His lusting love began

The woman of whispering white
Came in his dreams again
Drank of his body deep
The liquid taste of man.

Beyond Passion

Dawns each day I want her
Need her body so
Filling up my senses
Warming up my glow
Naked lovers lying long
Till the sun is high
Partners warm and willing
Until the day they die.

Take Me

Take me into your heart dear woman
Take me when I call
Take me into your heart dear woman
Take me should I fall
Take me into your mind dear woman
Take me into your head
Take me into your mind dear woman
As I lie on your bed.

Midlife Temptation

She came and sat beside me
Silky slim with long blonde hair
Racing pulse, my senses reeling
I felt a spark long since forgotten
Easy conversation, short lived joy
Alas we parted unfulfilled
But slumber came with dreams of pleasure
Pleasure only she could bring.

Enticing

———— ∞ ————

Evening long I watched her
Across that crowded room
Small and slender, so inviting
Eyes imploring, could be beckoning
Evening's end I sat beside her
Held her sweet young hand in mine
Bodies close desire so strong
Sex of Satan oh so wrong.

First Time

A spot of blood upon the dress
The one so white and clean
I wore it in the gym
Where you and I had been

You were so very gentle
When it did hurt a bit
And then I wanted more
The right spot you had hit

My unloved way had gone
With fumbling pushing so
Why I lost it then
I'm sure I do not know.

Lost Love

I kissed her in the morning
When the dew was on the rose
In a lover's leafy bower
Where sweet the jasmine grows

I loved her then as I do now
Her beauty does transcend
But I did lose her love
And pride shall never mend

Oft times I think of her
And feel her near to me
But now she's far away
In a land I'll never see.

The Land of Downy Dreams

Will you go with me by and by
To the land of downy dreams?
Where we shall lie as one
Warmed in the golden beams

I see you in that silken dress
Oft times I've seen before
Beckoning me come on do take
And I'm in your arms once more

I'm all around your body
My mind is in your head
Fine fusion of our beings
What more need there be said?

The Seeds of Barley Love

When the wind blows through the barley
My love and I shall meet
Where the barley fields grow plenty
There my love and I shall greet

Her scent is all around me
Teased tormented senses know
Urgent nakedness needs nurture
And this aching field I sow

And after in our later years
When we do meet more chaste
Untold memories flood our minds
Of the barley fields and haste.

My Lover's Eyes

Eyes that tell me everything
I ever wished to know
About this pleasing woman
I do worship so

Tonight I see their mischief
Reflected in her smile
Begs her body beautiful
Stay with me a while

And now the eyes are warmer
So close is she to me
Love transcends the passion
Of a union meant to be.

Before His Time

One hundred years before his time
A genius premature
Graced Victorian views
With poetry, prose and plays

A wit and brilliant raconteur
He courted Kings and Queens
An Irish classics scholar
Who lived to see his dreams

Troubled was his private life
His sexual preference puzzled
The need for manly company
So shocked that bygone world

Sodomite they called him
As they locked him up in jail
Where he wrote a splendid ballad
And called it Reading Gaol

Before his time was Oscar Wilde
Who paid for sexual choice
Today his bent is understood
Bisexuals have a voice.

Sexual Sleep

---∞---

Dreams of scarlet passion
Suffuse this sinful sleep
Flesh so full of longing
And desire for demons deep.

The Doubter

―――――― ∞ ――――――

For months the troubled thought
Be strong and throw him out
She knew not how to cope
With dreadful damning doubt

The word was infidelity
She knew it must be true
He was so much a woman's man
As all his lovers knew

Screwed up her rage inside
How could he so have been?
She swore she'd have revenge
Most manifest and mean.

The Proposal

That moment in the moonlight
When the stars were twinkling tears
And the clouds gone gliding by
To calm my nervous fears
I gazed upon that woman's face
And asked that she be mine
She did not nod nor did she speak
For me no outward sign
But the kiss that lingered long
On doubting lips of mine
Conveyed her message simply:
Accept what is divine.

The Concubine

———— ∞ ————

Command me to communicate
Insist that you should know
About an erstwhile concubine
Who wonders in your woe

I barely can remember
My youth except for when
I fondly favoured feelings
For a lovely I knew then

Had I felt like this before?
Her life seemed all for me
Features fair and feminine
All that I could see

Oh simple foolish youth
You cannot judge the mark
The wanton woman wandered
And found a better lark.

Doing It

Together
Finding flesh
You and I
Bodies intertwining
Sexual serpentining
Shiny soft skins
Soaked by salty sweat
Sliding symphonies
Glued sucking lips
Saliva seeking tongues
Accelerating rhythms
Peaks of panting pleasure
Escalate to ecstasy
Crashing comes crescendo
Soiling semen surge
Ends exhausted urge.

Union

———— ∞ ————

Then we are together
You and I complete
Sharing our emotions
Drinking in each one

Oh that woman softness
Your skin is made of silk
Pleasuring your womanhood
Our fusion quite complete

That bond twixt man and woman
To share a love so pure
Such biological passion
Forever shall endure

Love Me

Love me now
Love me then
Love me always
Love me when
Love my being
Love my soul
Love my aura
I don't know.

5
RELIGION

Circular God

The worship bell is ringing
An eager church to fill
Fearing faith the worthy go
Scorned those sinners sleep

The center of a circle
Like God and church as one
The radii the paths of life
So near or far from God

On line that rims the circle
A world of people walk
Beware beyond the circle
Where evil beast can stalk.

The Righteous are not Worthy

The righteous are not worthy
To tend the good Lord's feet
The bandages so soiled
By man spilled holy blood
That flowed from gaping holes
Where nails drove through the flesh
They pinned him perched up high
And took away his cause

He sparkled for the people
That very first Christmas day
He grew into a leader
And showed a world the way
Live the lesson of peace
And love each man and beast

At the feet of Jesus
Our lowly lives should be
Learn to care for others
And then we all shall see.

Mark of the Lord

Bending breaking the bread
Given by the child
Dripping like rain
Holy blood
His holy blood
From the thorn crowned head
Splashing that small cheek
There to remain
The mark of the Lord
A port wine stain.

Deliverance

Death is but a never-ending dream
Reflected in that final sleep
While all around do wailing weep
We our souls do creep
Beyond this transience we call living
To find utopia for the dead
Where God and angel hosts await
In this realm called eternity
Where chosen spectres dance divine
In limbo never more descending
To that soiled and spinning sphere
The world we know as earth
Can we poor creatures earthly born
Praise this greater being
Enough for deliverance
From that stinking world below
Where his mutant beast called man
Has done all in his power
To wreck the splendid creation
Of our dear lord god
By all the heinous devices
And more beside and in so doing
Sealed man's fate
Because god has decreed
That the earth shall be
Wrought asunder by his wrath

Which shall know no limit
No pity neither no mercy
And in the end
Man shall be naught
Then the supreme creator
Shall weeping wash away
What once was whole and good
And man no more shall stray.

Religious Question time

—————— ∞ ——————

Please don't think me irreverent
That's really not my style
It's just that I have questions
I've thought about a while

What are angels wings made of
And do they beat like birds?

Was Mary an adultress
Because she slept with God
Did Joseph feel the need
To show that he could breed?

Did Christ have sexuality
Or was he too devout?

And what of God himself
All powerful and all seeing
Does he answer to one above
Or is he the supreme being?

6
DEATH

The Yellow Crab

That sad old man
Sat nervously
Apprehensive
Waiting to hear
My pronouncing words
The most important words
He'd ever hear in his life

Strange that voice
My voice
A detailed explanation
How bad it really was
"Don't be alarmed"
My reassuring throw away
Sounded pathetic
But it's never easy
When life is the issue

Two months on
I sat with him
This man of yellow
Breathing barely
Rasping and rattling

The yellow crab
Would take him soon
It was always the way
And medicos could watch
And do nothing except
Move on to the next case...

Life after Death

The voices kept on calling
Join us please we pray
Floating free his soul
His body did obey

Gazing down from high
He viewed a corpse below
The body once was his
So dull and lifeless now

Past the place of death
A wall of light drew near
Like hapless moth be drawn
In and through beyond

A loving land of peace
He enters without fear
And feels the inner warmth
The afterlife must be

A sudden shudder jolting
Dragging dragging back
Through the wall of light
Through the deadly dark

The empty body greets him
Fleshing out his soul
Whole again he cheated death
That life so precious now.

A Time to Die

A mighty man his maker met
Time and date already set
No more his body racked by pain
Shall lie alone on bed again
A man of stature, wise as well
A foolish presence soon could tell
A father figure missed by all
To heaven his god soon must call.

The Mist of Birth and Death

Floating in from that giant pond
The mist mask made its creeping way
Over the beach, crawl climbed the pier
And silently cloaked the town from view

Cold and damp that night of mist
When homeless waifs lay out of doors
And one named Jenny birthed her last
A final gasp with her birthing heave

In her death blood did Jenny lie
A glazed dull eye of death exposed
The child lay helpless soon to die
An eerie cry did comfort crave

Nobody cared enough to save
This hapless pair on the streets
Who fought against the world of want
And died in the world of men.

Looking back from Death

The final days upon me
A time to die at last
My life always haphazard
Never making sense

Baby, child and man
Each a vital stage
Human moulding so
A mind and body match

Many days do I recall
When I did wish for death
Praying for better times
As sadness left my brain

Replaced by perfect pleasure
My world appeared to change
Kaleidoscopic colours
Brightened transiently

A roller coaster life
Extreme it must be said
Boundless energy
Or lying sad in bed

But now it matters little
I'm all reduced to dust
Death did take my flesh
And with it all my lust.

The Banyan Tree

———— ∞ ————

Bury me by the banyan tree
When surely I am dead
Cover me with soil
And let no more be said

Welcome roots grow in me
From soil and branch of tree
Absorbing my last fluids
The flesh at last set free

And still this banyan stands
So steadfast it must be
The branches, trunk and leaves
Are living growth from me.

The Latecomer

The Novak brothers told him
As he came off the train
Mother Howard died real sudden
She haemorrhaged in the brain

Old Bobby Howard was taken bad
He'd loved her like no other
Some folks say he's gone crazy
And time shall not recover

Gone the twins not two days old
Farmed out to great aunt Beth
Old Bobby couldn't bear to see
The ones who'd caused her death

The empty house without her
He'd once sat on her knee
God knows he owed her plenty
Her long lost son was he!

7
COLL

An Island Life

Oh to leave this island
Mainland set me free
For some a perfect heaven
For me a hanging tree

Treeless, tired and tatty
Thus it seems to me
Forever tinge my sadness
Lonely island of the sea

The youth are very active
Changing partners so
Often in euphoria
Pass the uppers Joe

Secting on the island
The older people know
Is their favourite pastime
And evil seeds they sow

Pigs are seldom seen
Utopia for the bad
Drivers do their thing
Unlawful it's so sad.

The swallows are the worst
Nesting transiently
No sooner come than gone
I wish they would take me.

Song of the Hebrides

Hail to the Hebrides!
That blot the western sea
Mysterious and magical
Forever they shall be.

Each island rich in beauty
Gazed by yachting sail
Floating with such majesty
Buffets fierce each gale

But what for me the Hebrides?
I know not why I care
Lonely sadness haunts me
Subdued the mood I wear.

Hangman's Hill

———— ∞ ————

Hangman's hill the dead man's hill
A mound with many a mood
Where the hanging noose upon the neck
For lucky few did break

But most in truth did strangulate
A slow and painful death
With open bowels and urine flow
Before that final gape

Hushed is hangman's hill today
For dead men make no sound
Bodies long since decomposed
Their spirits all around.

Gale Force Fathers

Wind of change
Great gusting gale
Forceful, fierce it blows

The pretty ones
Those bringers of joy
Gone are they now
From my safe harbour

Angry God and I
He with his breath
I my head

Howling roaring spitting
Downing
Bending breaking
Ripping tearing

Mean mood matching
Anger venting
With God's breath
Until at last
The calm of the fathers
Moderation brings.

Ponies

Brown and gray
The pair they lay
Content together
Huddled from the weather
Caring loving pair
On watchful world they stare

Shall they meander
In grassy green grandeur

Can do no wrong
So says the song
A song of mine
I know each line
An ancient tale
Of verdant dale
Where equine spirits live
No more to men shall give.

Near Departed Pooch

The world of dogs bereft?
Unthinkable tis so
The Kweli dog near gone
And Lorna laid so low

She loves her as a child
And rarely do they part
A soft spot for her pooch
Forever in her heart

Kweli's not for heaven
God won't let her in
I hope he has strong ears
She'll surely make a din!

Vein Drain

Of rustic bent
This soil tiller
Who bares his arm for me
No fear I sense
As tightening grip
I put around
To swell and bulge
Vein concealed warmth
In his rubor blood

Stinging the alcohol wipe
Precedes the needle point
Pricking his supple skin
Entering clean the vein
Dark red gushes forth
Tedious tubes to fill
Then out intruding needle
Leave his wounded vein
You shall not pierce again.

Oceana

Yon evening I did trip
To kiss the ocean's lip
Twas humid sans the nip
Me bared from toe to hip
That kiss might cost a slip
And I be forced to dip
While mermaids so do quip
You're in old Neptune's grip.

8
EGOCENTRICITY

I am no Mortal Man

Alone I stand on the bridge
The link that spans my life
Past lives to the right
The left my lives to live

Sensing gathering greatness
Speaks a voice in me
Envelop me in splendour
Immortal I shall be.

Demi God

He was a man of stature
A man of vision too
He fought for justice daily
With honour in his heart
No man dare ever doubt him
He seemed quite peerless then
As he strode among mere mortals
His will imposed on them.

Judgment

Come the final reckoning
Let all men say
That he, despite the imperfections
Would defend his cause to the end
And never give in to injustice
Nor not defend principles
And values he upheld
For surely every man
Who has integrity
Knows that such qualities
Are priceless possessions
Which set men apart
And mark them honourable.

9
HUMOROUS

Canine Woes

---∽---

Never did I like him
From that first moment on

Foul his breath from cigarettes
And drinking beer as well

A body huge and fearsome
His booming voice so loud

Kicking boots as big as boats
Shovel hands that push

Quick and quirky movements
He's such a manic man

Why does mummy like him?
Surely he should go

She takes him in her bed
They do what's very rude

I often try to join the group
But pushing hand is cruel

To punish for their badness
I bite and suck my feet

It doesn't seem to matter
All they do is sleep

Mummy gives me lots of treats
Chick chick and milky drinks

Sometimes she gives me pills as well
And checks I swallow them

I feel so sleepy after
They're very pleased I'm zonked

I plead and plead with mummy
Can you make him go?

She never gives an answer
But I'm sure it must be no.

Clicking and Whirring

Clicking and whirring through the day
Works so hard, gets no pay
Big and boring, coloured grey
Surplus wires, go away
Man made creature, need not pray
Abominal creation, threat today
What is it? Guess you may
Why my computer, here to stay!!!

Highlights

Always short and spiky
To show these pixie ears
An angry crop of rusty red
Foiled by pale pink skin

Craving change one day
While looking at her hair
She went to see her snips
Requesting highlight hints

Seeing her soon after
I gazed upon that mop
Subtle brownish highlights
Brushed on rusty locks

Somehow quite attractive
I tried hard not to stare
Those red hairs so put out
But highlights didn't care.

Bumblies Begone

Bumblies here, bumblies there
Dreadful bumblies everywhere
Bumbling into other's lives
As they do bumble on
But where are bumblies from
And what doth make them so
Oft times I've thought on it
And yet I do not know.

Helluva Heaven

Winging souls to heaven
Winging souls to hell
God anoints the saved ones
The devil tried to sell.

Green Horses

And there they were
Grazing contentedly
As if wondering
Why the fuss?
A field of equines
Big and small
Nothing very odd
Except they were GREEN
Some luminaire had said
The first few greenies
Had resulted from mating
Blue stallions with
Yellow mares
But everyone knows
There are no blue
Or yellow horses!
No one knew the answer
Perhaps God decided
To see what a green
Horse would look like
And then decided against
Because the next day
Those verdant creatures
Lovely in form
Were no more.

Time Travellers

———— ∞ ————

We don't know how he did it
But he built a time machine
And told the men from Baltimore
Who's names were never seen

The guns of Navarone were firing
At Turks and Persian boys
The Incas had to leave
They couldn't stand the noise

In France that very day
De Gaule met Joan of Arc
He put out her fire
And left her in the dark

Drake dropped his bowl
And Hitler held a Hun
Drake cried "Oh my foot"
While Hitler shot the nun

Darwin dined with Samson
After meeting with James Dean
They feasted on fowl species
But where had Jimmy been?

With all his men around him
Alexander could not get
He talked of global conquest
While he toyed with Antoinette

And then it was all over
He'd switched off the machine
Time travellers vortexed back
As if they'd never been.

10
AGE

Father of his Flock

Stooped and bent the body form
Short the shuffling gait
Rambling times so frequent now
A withered brain's last fate
Gone those days of purpose
The obsessions of the past
He was a very careful man
With skills in truth so vast.

Middle Years

Middle years were painful
Middle years so bad
Middle years were tearful
Middle years so sad.

Old with Experience

―――――――― ∾ ――――――――

Now that I am older
Some two score years and eight
How can I do those things
I did when twenty-one

Peering hard at near things
Forgotten are those specs
Or asking for a voice repeat
My hearing just can't cope

Mind less sharp than once
No memory is the crime
The body rather flabby now
Where once a tidy trim

Is there any saving grace
About this growing old?
The answer is experience
Great with age I'm told.

11

NARRATIVE

The Killer

The killer sat beside her
To journey on the train
He so full of killing
She of lovers fame

Consumed by so much hate
To kill was his intent
The knife hid in his coat
A fleshy sheath did seek

At last the train was still
The destination reached
His victim left the station
And a homeward route she took

So innocent in darkness
The woman makes her way
Her stalker seeks a place
There the evil deed to do

He follows down an alley
A perfect slaughter site
Sprinting brings him near
So eager now he'll kill

The grasping arm spins her round
And brings them face to face
Felt too late that evilness
That kills with plunging blade

His hatred all but spent
He pulls the weapon free
Then tender kissed the dead lips
The darkness sets him free.

Supper for the Sharks

—————— ∞ ——————

Far and wide
The sky was blue
The sea electric green
The pirate ship
Upon the waves
With such a cut throat crew

None to a man did tell
How scar faced Johnny
Let out the breath
Yon customs man at Leith
So deep he stabbed the chest
And hissing air let out

But Johnny he was cornered
He'd done an awful thing
Did drink the captain's brandy
Then guzzled down the gin
His penalty to walk the plank
The captain's word was law

The sea of sharks awaits
Johnny eyes with pain
As he walks along the plank
A sword point pricks his back
Too quick the end is reached
And Johnny forced to leap

A frenzied turmoil boils
A sea of blood and foam
The screaming flesh is ripped
Those sharks will have their fill
Our Johnny's surely done for
No second man he'll kill.

War Words

Gone are all the flowers now
Drowned in a sea of blood
Where a thousand men lie bleeding
And a thousand more lie dead

Close to death a soldier lies
Scenes of battle crowd his mind
Sees the horses charging charging
Screaming men, grunting pain
Fallen horses, fallen men
Fighting soldiers, hand to hand
Death so sudden, death so slow
Crashing cannons boom again
Tearing and ripping men apart
Bits of pieces all that's left

Now the soldier near to death
Full of peace, full of grace
Hears a voice, beckoning so
Heaven be yours for ever more.

12
MISCELLANEOUS

The Wahine

───── ∞ ─────

Wet to waist the wahine
Waddled up the beach
Left the lonely fishing boat
Dragged out of the sea

Hair black to the waist
Adorned with flowers so fresh
Plump and plain the face
Baked and brown the skin

Simple white the blouse
A floral skirt clung wet
Fleshy fish her catch
Quivering hung from waist

Greetings as she passed
In a strange and southern tongue
A figure seen of this land
Where her proud life began.

A Sort of Justice

Mute and sad upon the bough
Dangling legs the water seek
Beneath the floating lily pads
Cool currents calm her woes

White the shrouding dress
A mask of gloom her face
Sweet the lap of flowers
Her grave shall they adorn

What is this troubling past?
That leaves you so distressed
Did dying lover take your mind?
When you his life did end.

Birth of a Parasite

Warm and wet contentment
Floating in the womb
Parasitic parent abuse
Maternal heart approves

Forty wet weeks on
Sensing birthing time
Forcing vault did push
Like piston driving through

To face this lighted land
A life so raw and real
To join with other men
And walk this planet earth.

Rivers of Rain

Rivulets of water
Rivers running rain
Racers wet the glass
Vying for a lane

Eager for the win
Jostling all the way
Anger in their pain
Death to die today.

Vernal Verve

———— ∞ ————

I feel the strength of spring
Suffuse my dullard brain
That snoozed away the winter
With lazy body frozen out
Till liquid spring wells up
To end old winter's wear
And fill all eyes with sight
Of verdant land once more

Singing songs of spring
The avians of this time
When living breathing forms
Depart their winter woes
To feel such vernal verve
Lift their spirits so
Neither knowing whence it came
Nor wanting it to go.

Dry Surfing

Weird the wires of wonder
Like spider web that knows
The communicating network
Where all reality goes

One thirty million websites
Never two the same
Html is the language
To surf it is the game.

He Was Never Right

———— ∞ ————

No he was never right

Never right for me

Never right for the job

Too much twitching

Too much shaking

A nervous soul

Spluttering so

There were times

I even pitied

But then he started

Droning on

By way of compensation

Boring without insight

On some wretched subject

Unaware his "listeners"

Had switched off

Thinking cheerily

Of everything but him

Sometimes rage

After all my

Non-subtle cues

Had failed

Would all but steel

Me to say

You sir are

The most boring

Buffer I say

Of course I never did

Where is he now?

Gone from me

Gone from my job

Some say he is

Where Welsh hearts dwell

Dragons await

Breathing hell.

Oak Hearts

Pray for me when I am gone
From this pleasant land
Where soft winds blow
The leaves that cloak
Those mighty trunks

The oak filled hearts
Tall ships did build
Now nestling in the bay

Too soon those ships
As fleet shall sail
Out of that gentle bay
To strike a blow

For liberty

And ever after
That destruction day
Shall be remembered
Some shall weep
Most will thank
For such deliverance.

The Singing Poet

Who is this man
Who writes and sings
The poetry of life?
I heard him first
When but a youth
He truly set me free
With music poetry
Words so sweet
Forever part of me

A helping of American pie
An anthem for the young
New words and phrases
For their world
So willingly they come

Starry starry night
A canvas of a song
About poor Vincent's beauty
Yes they got it wrong
He showed them how to listen
In tune with artist's ear
Now starry's loved by all
His painting without peer

Don Mclean I praise you
You spread the music word
A world without your poetry
Unthinkably absurd.

Oppression

And the mist came down
To lie on the ground
Like some great blanket
Made of woven water
To chill the earth
And wet its skin
Yet still those claymored men
Charged forward in waves
To be shredded
By sworded cavalry ranks
Of the arrogant English
Who had and would go on
Oppressing proud Scotland
Until the last drop
Of blood from the last
Scotsman was shed
Twas clear that this fight
Was an English day
A foregone conclusion
And yet the Scots
Are proud and shall
Never yield to tyranny
Nor its like
Did we not keep
The Roman dogs at bay?
When all proud England

Overrun by them
Scotland shall have her day
Mark me well I say
And such a fine day
When all of Alba
Shall rejoice
A shout of freedom
So loud shall deafen
And waken the dead
Aye Wallace and Bruce
Shall know of this day
When Scotland is reborn
Proud and free.

Portrait of a Painter

Never pretty
That face
Too angular
Fierce and frightening
Hair of fiery red
Severely cropped
The near full beard
Darker red and tangled
A shabby habit
Completes this picture
Of a man with little
And naught to offer
This material world
Where owning is all

And yet there is something
Yes in the eyes
So deep set
Beady and brown
Piercing
Deep within is sensitivity
Perhaps creativity

Now he paints
All is clear
The brush lives
An extension of him
Those bristles his senses
Making his music
Painting perfection

Oh Vincent
How could I ever doubt you?
I look on your work
And marvel
A peerless painter
We shall not see thy like again.

Window of Hope

In the distance
So very far away
Can it be?
A window hope for me
But wait
Is it open?
Yes!
Now I can see
Beyond is blue and beautiful
Horizons new for me.

About the Author

George Carle was born at his father's farm in Aberdeenshire on the twelfth of February nineteen fifty-two. He was the youngest of four children and somewhat spoilt. He attended Kininmonth primary school and Peterhead Academy for his secondary education. He was an achiever at school and attended Aberdeen University where he studied Medicine, graduating in nineteen seventy-six. He pursued a career in General Surgery and was elected a Fellow of the Royal College of Surgeons of Edinburgh in nineteen eighty-one. Soon after this he spent a year in Boston, Massachusetts, studying Surgical Nutrition. After working for a spell in Ophthalmology his career moved to General Practice. For many years he worked in a large English Practice near Doncaster before moving to his present location, the Isle of Coll.

He started writing poetry two years ago after an acute and traumatic separation from his wife and family. Self described as a sensitive and creative poet, he believes—like Hardy—that poetry should be written when charged with emotion. His poetry has a traditional slant and a minimalist style. The many subjects covered include emotional distress, death, his dear children, religion, age, humour, separation and love. He has written well over one hundred and fifty poems and many have been accepted for publication and a number are published in well-known poetry magazines and anthologies.

The Isle of Coll is a remote and isolated inner Hebridean island where the author has lived for four years. A regular ferry service connects with the mainland. The island boasts a population of approximately one hundred and sixty though summer visitors expand this number significantly. The island has unspoilt beauty and provides an ideal setting for the doctor-poet to compose some truly wonderful verse.

9 780595 162741

27744540R00095

Printed in Great Britain
by Amazon